My Shabby Afterlife

My Shabby Afterlife

Poems by

Aaron Fischer

© 2022 Aaron Fischer. All rights reserved.
This material may not be reproduced in any form, published,
reprinted, recorded, performed, broadcast,
rewritten or redistributed without
the explicit permission of Aaron Fischer.
All such actions are strictly prohibited by law.

Cover design by Shay Culligan
Cover collage by Lauren Rowland
Rear cover painting of author by Lauren Rowland

ISBN: 978-1-63980-153-4

Kelsay Books
502 South 1040 East, A-119
American Fork, Utah 84003
Kelsaybooks.com

For Lauren Rowland

Other books by Aaron Fischer

Black Stars of Blood: The Weegee Poems

Ted Berrigan: An Annotated Checklist

Journal of the Plague Years

The Wild Cherry

Acknowledgments

My thanks to Marty Lampner, Neal Meltzer, and Peter Perez for never caring if I wrote a poem.

And to Kim Addonizio and Ellen M. Stevenson for making sure I did.

I am deeply grateful to the editors of the following journals where some of these poems were first published, sometimes in earlier versions:

Adelaide Literary Journal: "Lines for Joey Ramone," "Speed Freaks (Buffalo, NY 1969)," "Oranges and Lemons," "Ferry to Hart Island," "Tourist Cabins Loon Lake (1959)"

After Happy Hour Review: "Plague and Rumor"

The American Journal of Poetry: "Color by Number Picture of Auschwitz," "The Big Jew," "Close Harmony: The Louvin Brothers," "Venice"

The Briar Cliff Review: "Elegy for SKM"

The Brownstone Poets 2020 Anthology: "Stray Thoughts for Viktor Schlovsky"

Columbia Poetry Review: "Huffing"

Crosswinds Poetry Journal: "Near-Death Experience," "Reverend Gary Davis Live at Newport"

The Ekphrastic Review: "Soutine's Still Life with Rayfish"

Evening Street Review: "Thank You for Your Service," "On His Deafness"

Five Points: "Last Laugh"

Hamilton Stone Review: "Expatriate Elegy," "Moonrise from a Balcony in Brooklyn," "Lust for Life (MGM: 1956)," "Guide to New Jersey," "Night Piece: New Jersey"

Naugatuck River Review: "Days of 1981," "Lives of the Saints (Flatbush, 1967)"

Prime Number Magazine: "Howlin' Wolf at the Fillmore East, June 7, 1968," "Crazy Eights"

Tishman Review: "Long Point Lake"

"Crazy Eights" won the 2020 Prime Number Magazine Award for Poetry. "Howlin' Wolf at the Fillmore East, June 7, 1968" was a finalist in the 2017 contest.

"Aubade for LR" was chosen as a 2018 Sonnet of the Year by the Maria W. Faust Sonnet Contest. "Fats Waller: Living Large" won in 2021.

Contents

Bucket List	15
Close Harmony: The Louvin Brothers	16
Long Point Lake	18
Tourist Cabins Loon Lake (1959)	20
Who Has Seen the Wind?	21
Near-Death Experience	22
Moonrise from a Balcony in Brooklyn	23
John Clare's Birds	24
B&W: The Beatles at the Cavern Club	25
Albrecht Dürer: *Self-Portrait at 26* (1498)	26
Lives of the Saints (Flatbush 1967)	30
Speed Freaks (Buffalo, NY 1969)	31
Huffing	32
Mutability Canto	34
White Rabbit (Jefferson Airplane)	35
Venice	36
Lines for Joey Ramone	38
A Word from Our Sponsors	41
The Queen's English	42
Man at Work	45
The Big Jew	46
A Jew on a Picnic	47
Triptych for MKF	48
Rose Mallow	48
Plein-Air	49
Plein-Air (again)	50
The Joys of Yiddish	51
Color by Number Picture of Auschwitz	55
The Recording Angel	56
Google Earth View of the House I Grew Up In	57
Stray Thoughts for Viktor Schlovsky	62
Rolling Stock for Marty Lampner	63
Fax Machine Receives Message from God	64

Ferry to Hart Island	65
Lust for Life (MGM: 1956)	66
Swallowtail and Killing Jar	67
This Call May Be Recorded for Quality-Assurance Purposes	69
Link Wray: One-Hit Wonder	70
Homage to Samuel Johnson: 17 Gough Square	73
Days of 1981	75
Expatriate Elegy	77
In Memoriam: SKM	78
Crazy Eights	79
Clamdiggers	80
A Love Supreme	81
My Shabby Afterlife	83
Last Laugh	84
Howlin' Wolf at the Fillmore East, June 7, 1968	85
Plague and Rumor (NY 1980)	87
Soutine's *Still Life with Rayfish*	88
Guide to New Jersey	89
Feral Parrots, New Jersey	90
Fort Hudson, New Jersey	91
Night Piece: New Jersey	92
Suburban Sonnet	94
Shakespeare in South Jersey	95
Fats Waller: Living Large	97
Baltimore Christmas: Remembering Uncle Beanie	98
Thank You for Your Service	99
On His Deafness	100
Night Blindness	101
Reverend Gary Davis: Live at Newport	102
Oranges and Lemons	103
Aubade for LR	104

Bucket List

I'd like to meet a woman inked with a blurred,
blue line from one of my poems, the words a bit
muzzy—they've been under her skin long enough
for time to temper regret, without forgetting

they took their toll in blood. Not some dewy
millennial with Kool-Aid-hued hair,
a technicolor sleeve of Saturday-
morning cartoons I'm sure I watched before

she was born. The supermarket's a better bet,
someone bagging groceries, a familiar phrase
snaking beneath a sleeve, someone restocking

shelves on the lobster shift, muscling pallets
of baby food, that chiseled couplet reduced
to something like a birthmark or a bruise.

Close Harmony: The Louvin Brothers

one

Nothing sounds as sweet as blood singing
to blood, brother to brother, their voices

closely woven as strands of rope,
Ira's come-to-Jesus tenor riding

Charlie's honky-tonk lower register,
until they were one voice, aching and pure,

delivering the bad news preached by holy rollers—
sin and death, guilt and remorse,

the long shot at redemption
promised in smoky, kerosene-lit tent revivals.

"Are You Ready to Die," they sang, "Satan is Real,"
sounding as if they knew hell firsthand.

two

They tortured Nashville's weepy standards
into three minutes of heartache and agony,

into a regular slot on the Grand Ole Opry
singing about love as if it were another kind

of damnation—*In the pines, in the pines,
where the sun never shines...* The pedal steel

pleading and skirling just out of reach
of Ira's range, as much mockery as accompaniment,

as if love were a splinter in the palm of his hand,
and it was the job of the song to dig it out.

three

Backstage at the Opry, Ira chases
pills with Johnny Walker Black, curses

his three ex-wives and spendthrift fourth,
can't tune his mandolin, breaks it across his knee.

(Sober, or nearly so, he'll rock and keen
over the pieces.) Charlie won't talk to him

offstage or on, stares at a point just above
the heads of the audience. Ira's got

five years before a drunk driver
kills him head on, his sleek-finned Caddy

reduced to scrap. Charlie will live 30 more
never forgiving himself for not forgiving his brother,

knowing the job of a song is to leave a scar.

Long Point Lake

All day north, until there was nothing
on the radio but the whisper and seethe

of static—the fossil music of the universe
running out of time—and nothing

on the TV in the tiny house we took
for a week to work on our marriage, except

coarse snow ghosting across the screen.
"Let's leave it on," I said, flipping the channels,

"in case we run out of things to say."
We were so young we thought we could talk

our way to happiness, thought
the sullen spats about having kids,

or counseling, or buying a house
were just a rough patch.

We were too timid to ask for what we needed,
in bed or out. You had to be half drunk

before you let me go down on you.
I was ashamed to say I wanted you

in heels and garters like the women
in the magazines I kept stashed in my desk.

All those words like the slow skeins of smoke
curling from the cabins on the other shore.

What I remember are the Canada Geese
flying out of the sun into their reflections

on the water, strafing the lake with shit—
the night you bit and hissed at my ear,

"Hold me down," scissoring your legs around
my waist, "isn't this what you really want?"

while V after V of birds squadroned
over the roof, filling the room

with their liquid barking, while the shadows
on the TV, like hikers lost in a blizzard,

warped and rippled under the glass.

Tourist Cabins Loon Lake (1959)

In one, the faint tang of mildew and bleach informed
our sleep, in another, an archipelago of mossy stains
bloomed on the wallpaper—those tourist cabins my parents
rented for a week in August, when Brooklyn shimmered

like a fever dream, when my mother in her dust-colored
robe, and my father, bedded down on the couch in his BVDs,
forged their sullen, seasonal ceasefire. *Money, money, money*
sniggered the window fan, troubling the dead air.

The lake glittered, a sheet of tin. My mother burned,
my father browned. I sat on the porch, afraid of the sugar-drunk
yellowjackets loaded on Kool-Aid. Under the sun-dazzled
trees the leaf-filtered light made me think of coins, scattered

for a brother and sister to follow into the forest
until they found a house good enough to eat.

Who Has Seen the Wind?

Where was it headed in such a hurry, eager
to be anywhere but this dead-end street, battering
the tall reeds in their drab winter wear,
their sad browns and russet, bruising

the last color from the salt marsh, violet, magenta
rippling across the windrows, as hard to hold in the eye
as an afterimage? Memory's like that: there,
not there—the way two hammers will suddenly

synch up when carpenters frame a house. A family
moves in, with its thrift-shop linen, its hard-luck
heirlooms: the mother gray and blank as a test pattern,

the father, promising they can get by
on fix-it work—blown tubes and schematics, the burnt-sugar
scent of solder rising through the heat vents.

Near-Death Experience

The baffling tunnel, the bruising
light, like surfacing in the blinding OR, while the surgeon
watches your heart stutter, and the dear departed mill
about in a mob, waiting for a glimpse of the condemned:

my salutatorian mother in her refugee
drag—men's shoes, Goodwill flannel and houndstooth—
my aunt, grown enormous on her regimen
of antipsychotics, my father's huge mitts hanging loose

at his side for once. Jewish gothic. Did they love me
enough? Claustrophobically: the windows sealed all winter
with plastic, a pan of blues or stripers
smoking on the stove. When the wind scaled the crazy-

quilt shingles off the roof I swore I'd get out,
living or dead I'd never come home.

Moonrise from a Balcony in Brooklyn

for Anna Fischer and Philip Kalmes

Slowly, deliberately as a Kennedy half
magic'd from a silk top hat, the full moon
clears the banked clouds shrouding Staten Island,
where the mob once ran

the world's biggest garbage dump—Fresh Kills,
that irony surely lost on no one,
the gulls stacked up like air traffic over JFK,
wheedling and crying like penitents.

In this green era the trash heaps and hummocks are lush
as lawns. Whatever light the cloud cover allows
silvers nature walks, bike paths,

the blind for watching shorebirds. But the gulls
are up to the same thuggish tricks year-round:
bullying each other to drop their scraps.

John Clare's Birds

Where go the swallow tribes?

They're just as much about danger and death—
the undersongs in all his poems—as they are
about his cherished birds: the winter fowler,
his pockets stuffed with crumbs to draw the thrush

to slaughter, village boys plundering nests,
and cats of course—*grimalkin*—the fossil word
he chose because he spoke the dialect
of pure isolation. I think those birds

were his poems, *a wild and timid clan,* or Clare
himself, the peasant poet, helped and hurt
into the madhouse (gentle for the age)

when progress first curdled his home landscape,
silencing spring's luminous green patchwork,
melodious fields with birdsong everywhere.

B&W: The Beatles at the Cavern Club

By now the club's a sacred site, this out-
of-focus, barrel-vaulted cellar, dank
Victorian brickwork long out-of-plumb,
too damp to lean against, the kids crammed in,
emptying local shops and family firms
at lunchtime, girls in aerosol-enhanced
bouffants or lacquered beehives, boys turned out
in Cuban heels and stovepipes, music loud
enough to find and fill the empty space
in each of them. The lads are still in jeans
and leather, like the hitters they never
were. Sitting behind his secondhand drum kit
Pete Best tries out his brood and pout, as if
he's posing for a cover shoot. The rest
have only started growing into their
famous names and faces. Something's about
to happen to them beyond imagining,
the way a flash at ground zero in a cold-
war sci-fi film ripples around the world.
Something's about to change us all, though who
could argue now it was for the best.

Albrecht Dürer: *Self-Portrait at 26* (1498)

one

Perhaps a better title, "Portrait of
a Dandy": Dürer's Age of Aquarius

cascade of curls and ringlets breaks below
his shoulders—dirty blond and loosely crimped—

a scruffy-soulful beard and moustache frame
a small, ungenerous mouth, surprisingly so,

considering his extravagant attire—
"effeminate grace," one critic sniped, though

"luxurious" is more than equal to
the task: the doublet, Italian silk, in cream,

its cuffs and collar edged in black, with stripes
in black as well, shaping the sleeve so we

can feel the weight and mass of the arm inside,
a pleated linen shirt trimmed with gold lace.

This costume drama's more to Dürer than
a chance to preen. It shows his patrons what

they get for their guilders: a hand adept
enough to render what his eye discerns,

the way the subtle-shaded shadows brim
and fade along the cloak's ridges and folds

or vanish where the window admits
the northern light, the way each tassel on

the striped, foppish cap can be stroked and traced,
its plush weight confirmed.

two

Did Dürer even own the clothes he brushed
on canvas, or were they worked in watercolor
and gouache, a study sketched in a notebook

carried home from Venice, that confection
of limestone, gold, and glass that held the key—
he wrote to Willibald, his oldest friend—

to all he set himself to master: line,
perspective, proportion, and man's image?
Or did he hire a narrow, sleek gondola

that barely creased the water, putting in
at the island where the tailors lived and worked,
the light suffused with water, bolts of cloth—

macaw green, indigo, vermilion—some
few meant only to grace the bluest bloods,
the princes of the church. Germany was

home, Nuremburg, the Brenner Pass carved across
the Alps. It's spring or early summer, the steep,
sparse pastures gentian-starred, diagonals

of foxglove, heartsease—cloud-rippled coral,
electric blue. (We have his luminous
watercolors.) And what of his ornate,

Venetian garb, his over-the-top glad rags?
Stowed in his trunk, a sachet (rosemary
and lilac, black peppercorns) to dispel

the canals' bouquet, their funk of brine and filth?
But what if there were no astonishing
wardrobe, no turn and turn about before

the tall cheval glass, and no tailor, for
that matter, an idea, nothing more
and nothing less, when he was waved inside

the arched tower gate into this city
of winter fogs, with its impoverished
daylight all through the coldest months?

three

All portraits lie. Self-portraits most of all.
Despite his haute bourgeois habiliments,

his upper-middle-class apparel, Dürer knew
he was just a working stiff to patrons

and burghers alike—clever the way a cobbler
or carpenter had to be to satisfy

clients and wives. The gulf between the ones
who worked with hands and those with heads—accountants

to the right, grease monkeys to the left—was set
in stone, and Dürer's woodcuts, "St. Jerome,"

"The Passion," only proved the point, despite
his books on shadows and strategy. "Here,

I am a gentleman, at home only
a parasite." His dirty little secret.

He's wearing gloves—one cuff turned up—in this
elusive masterpiece, the oblong moons

of his fingernails etched in the soft leather.
If he had left one off, would there be scars

where chisels slipped, the burin skidded on
the copper plate, shaming indictments, proof

that labor was his element?

Lives of the Saints (Flatbush 1967)

At 15, I wanted to be a saint, an odd
preoccupation for a gawky, bookish Brooklyn Jew,
head full of Ginsberg, head full of glue,
more in love with Dylan and Hendrix than God.

The miracles were window dressing: St. Martin
touching the choking boy's throat with a cross.
Francis regaling the rapt birds. Even Lazarus,
waking to the abrupt light, still in his cerement.

How they tutored me in renunciation,
those penitents who broke their epic fasts
with water by the thimbleful, scraps

of stale bread. How I courted starvation,
the way it made me feel clean, the way
each time I stood the world darkened and swayed.

Speed Freaks (Buffalo, NY 1969)

It was the winter of yellow jackets and black beauties—
diet pills loose in a bowl like Halloween candy, Chick's trailer
half buried in drift scattershot with scurf and cinder
blown downwind from our neighbor Mohawk Steel and Foundry.

It was the winter my mouth always tasted of blood,
when we lived on Benzedrine, Tang, and toast,
and never went out before the sun slid behind the hoists
and razor wire fencing the steelyard.

That was the winter I dropped out of school.
Chick caught pneumonia and tried
walking to the VA hospital, until the cops picked him up on I-90,

wearing an army blanket over his camo fatigues,
the winter he swapped my picture for the blurry face of the lost kid
asking, "Have you seen me?" on a carton of curdled milk.

Huffing

It's almost impossible to keep the glue
off us and in the brown paper bag,
one of those little lunch bags
kids carry, but primed with a tube of glue—

star splotches on our hands, cold
residue in Leanne's mouth
when she brings her mouth
to mine, raising her face from the bag, cold

wow-and-flutter of my heart as it down-
shifts, stutters, and slows,
cigarette smoke looping and uncoiling in slo-mo
or free falling like a hang glider in a down-

draft, and I see we're made of nothing
but time—background music for a hall of mirrors,
last thing you hear when death holds its mirror
to your lips and you become nothing.

Leanne takes her top off last, breasts
branded with small scars,
cigarette burns, matchheads—scars,
along her collarbone above her breasts,

as if she needed a wound to make herself real,
to keep from vanishing,
while I thought vanishing
was the point, becoming less and less real,

like a cicada husk clinging to the whorled
face of a leaf: amber and supremely absent,
the way a saint must be absent
who renounces the world.

Leanne unzips my jeans, wants me to hurt her
back into herself, but I'm too deep
in the bag to get hard, too deep
on the nod to help her

We lie on the gutted couch, side by side,
stuffing spilling out like seafoam,
breathing and trembling like seafoam,
while the dark pools and rises outside.

Mutability Canto

Asking was it a different city then
is almost a koan. What stays the same?
the fractal burst of pigeons settling down

again on park benches? the sharp savor
of coriander, cumin, lamb, and saffron
braiding and unbraiding from the food carts

in Midtown, shifting as the wind shifts?
Memory's worse. For all its attention
to detail, it can't sustain a storyline.

An orange cat asleep in a bookshop window,
an admin in a Maxfield Parrish pose,
barefoot and slim, catching some rays at lunch,

a pattern, if there is one, coded and obscure
as those shadow letters banding the cat's fur.

White Rabbit (Jefferson Airplane)

"You need to embrace the freak out," advice from GB, circa 1970

As much as inner weather, music is
a kind of muscle memory: *White Rabbit,*

the snare and bass rough out a parade-ground riff
the guitar ignores for something—Arabic?—

some trippy fragment heard off-world. Our breath
silvers the car windows, my fingers laced

through Smitty's densely coiled blond curls, her head
between my legs, a gram of opiated

hash smoked to soot. But Grace carries the song,
Grace Slick, her arctic voice urging another

tab of acid, line of blow, fashioning
a chill wonderland. Why were we so eager

to dare the rabbit hole?—DD and Sluggo,
Wes and Smitty, her skin like the moon on snow.

Venice

Like most dreams this one is best
approached by water, the flat-bottomed boat
throwing no more wake than a gondola, the rusty outboard
killed to a cough and whisper, a pennant of blue smoke,
Caton Ave. brimming with glassy shadows and light,
as if it were the Grand Canal, as if Brooklyn were Venice.

I'm looking for you, Katya,
but you're not waiting for me
at one of the wobbly white wicker tables
in front of Rudy's Authentic New York Pizza, wearing
your coppery hair in a French braid,
French inhaling a cigarette because it gives Angelo
the busboy a hard-on.

You're not shoplifting 45s at the Record Riot
in a poodle skirt and Doc Martens, counting on the manager
to pay more attention to your legs
than the Ray Charles single tucked in your bag,
and laughing when he throws you out.

You're not scoring a dime bag of smack from Chilly Willy,
teasing him about the diamond in his tooth,
showing him where you pierced your nose
one night with a needle and an ice cube
to make you look more gypsy than Jew.

****

We were going to Venice you announced—
hair turbaned in a damp towel—
waving a National Geographic stolen from the library
where the woman at the circulation desk had a crush on you.

Once a year, we learned, the city marries the sea,
the ceremony half Mardi Gras, half high mass,
the serried, double-prowed gondolas, an old man
with the face of a tipsy bureaucrat dressed
in brocade and red silk like a Renaissance pope.

You loved ritual and mystery—laying out the tarot,
Death and The Lovers, the tenebrous
interiors and rose windows of the churches
along Albemarle and Linden.

****

The first time you OD'd
I slid an ice cube up your ass, ran a tub of cold, rusty water
and kept you from drowning.

The last time I saw you we rode the D train all night,
both of us junk-sick, your arms tattooed with bruises.
I begged you to go to rehab.

The dream knows more than the dreamer
you told me in a dream. I've given up
listening for the harsh bray of your laughter,
more crow than queen, you said.

When you married the ocean,
when your gilded funeral barque
set out in the choppy mouth of the Adriatic,
did the gondoliers balance the long blades
of their oars straight up and down in tribute?

Lines for Joey Ramone

(Jeffery Ross Hyman, 1951–2001)

When the last words of some conversation
get lost in a spatter of crackle and buzz, I can almost hear again

the band roaring through its set, the music palpable
as a windstorm, pushing the crowd back half a step,

cranking up the slam-dancers in the mosh pit,
as if the floor of CBGBs were a hot skillet,

while you prowl the cramped stage—leather jacket, skinny
jeans, black high-tops—dragging the mic stand

behind you like it's attached to an IV,
or jump up and down, fist pumping,

hair falling over your face and shades,
a scrawny punk afflicted with St. Vitus Dance.

****

In the summer of my lost year,
under the signs of the roach and silverfish,

the Lower East Side collapsing on its own
into rubble and plaster dust,

the music was all we wanted, the drugs
were just something to do while waiting,

we told ourselves, like the great jazzmen, the dead
soldiers—sticky-sweet Robitussin empties—

piling up in the sink, the crimped tubes of glue
and paper bags littering the floor of the bedroom,

the Mexican heroin the club kids sold,
black tar, the scraps of tinfoil used to chase the dragon.

There was always another show. At the Continental
and Max's, at Coney Island High on St. Marks,

at the Mudd Club and the Pyramid, where the bartenders
wore full drag and earplugs while the band

howled through its cover of "Palisades Park"
and you delivered your surreal catchphrases,

like "Gabba Gabba Hey," which we loved
because it meant nothing, just as we loved you,

an acne-pocked kid from Queens with bad teeth,
our goofy virtuoso of chaos.

****

It took me three shots at rehab to get it right.
I moved to Jersey and worried for years

I would run into someone I knew at the Chinese takeout
or laundromat. I bought each record

when it came out: The band getting louder, like a chop shop
dismembering Hondas and Toyotas on Ave D,

the songs faster, your frayed voice giving out
on the choruses. When did you know you were dying?

I saw your last show at the Academy of Music,
your Christmas spectacular. You looked as if

you were leaning back against that wall of sound,
letting it buoy and buffet you, and the audience,

frightened into an awkward tenderness,
tried to sing along.

A Word from Our Sponsors

When the black & white world was on the cusp
of living color, TV commercials couldn't get

enough of cute, corporate avatars—Speedy Alka Seltzer,
the Pillsbury Doughboy. I loved them as much

as Saturday morning cartoons, singing along
with their advertising jingles, those tiny arias.

No wonder nostalgia has its hooks in us,
the way it transforms kitsch into fetish and talisman.

The Greeks believed memory was mother of the muses.
I can get behind that, when it means the starfield

of fireflies L and I found flickering in the tall grass,
my children's slick heads crowning the birth canal,

but what comes to mind just as readily—a dented
Flintstone's lunchbox, a gleaming plastic bayonet.

The Queen's English

There were the usual immigrant mysteries
concerning my great-aunt, not why she fled
the Pale, that pen the czar decreed to keep
his Jews on hand for pogroms, Eastertide

roundups for blood libel, but which miasmal,
pig-stupid shtetl she'd left behind, the sky
deep-seeded with stars that likely meant little
to her or less: There's no place for Semite

virgins or pretty-boys along the zodiac.
I never thought to ask about her name
until L wondered after the funeral how

a nice Jewish boy from Brooklyn's favorite
aunt was his aunt Regina, saying it made
me sound as if I should have prepped at Holy

Trinity, worn a blazer, joined Latin
club. Sneaking a smoke behind the boys' gym
at Sacred Heart, pomade and mauve sharkskin,
a better bet—with sisters, cousins, prim

aunts all called after the queen of heaven.
It's a familiar story among Jews
who chose or were given American
names almost as soon as they came through

Ellis Island, so eager to show they deserved
their place, to prove untrue old-country tropes
that arrived ahead of them and warned we were

deceitful, grasping, cliquish, cheap, and over-
sexed. In Yiddish, her dying *mamaloshen*—
her mother tongue—my aunt would have answered

to *Malke,* queen, an easy reach to Regina
for anyone with a smattering of church
Latin. The transfiguration of my father's
cousin *Yonkele* to John Kelly, a punch-

line that couldn't be bettered. Bogus, all
these greenhorn sea changes, this steerage folklore.
The halt, the sick, the ulcerous and palsied,
polygamists, unmarried mothers were

immigration's bread and butter. Anarchists
and lungers. Otherwise, the new world waited,
after the guards compared your name against

the passenger list. Did *Malke* come aboard
in Bremerhaven, later finding it
prudent for reasons unknown to adopt

an assumed name? Or was it Regina who
crowded on deck when tugs bullied and nudged
the ship into the harbor to see the Statue
of Liberty, her copper robes the color

of a tarnished penny? She could only be one
or the other on her chilly North Atlantic
crossing. Why does my tribe recount fictions
in which we're neither brave nor brilliant?

Or were they meant to teach survival skills
to exiles whose homes were whirlwind and fire?
We remain ourselves, we remain ourselves,

despite disguises the world demands we wear.
A final puzzle: Her English was pitch-perfect,
beyond the rote sing-song, the useful words,

the point-and-speak vocabulary drilled
in night classes at Henry Street Settlement.
Her youngest sister, my grandmother, still
said *telewision,* unable to shake the accent

that was as much her as the lukewarm, canned
pineapple juice she served with dinner. My
brother and I spoke a patois part Brooklyn,
part lower-middleclass burb, where *lorndry*

and *warsh* were hung on the line. I asked. And again.
That was so very long ago, she said,
still keeping secrets. I only heard her voice

once more, the Workmen's Circle on Audubon,
a nursing home for old socialists,
a block away from where Malcolm X

was killed. She was dozing, and when she woke
didn't know me, hovering as she was
between worlds—dead and living, new and old.
I'm Jack and Marjorie's son, your niece Marge.

She fell asleep holding my hand, waking
when a nurse, carafe and evening meds balanced
on a tray told me tomorrow, visiting
hours started at two, after our guests eat lunch.

When I bent to kiss her she asked again,
Who are you? I offered my brief bio. *Thank you
for coming to see me, but you're not Aaron.*

Man at Work

The only time my father had the cash
to drive a new car off a dealer's lot

his shyster cousin finagled seven grand
for him after a fender bender, just

for wearing a collar brace and seeing
a specialist, though not until he'd been prepped

about the shooting pains and aching knee.
(My friends and I took most of the Darvocet.)

Among my father and his friends, coming
up short was chronic. The boxy tub he chose

came loaded—factory air, power windows—
but idled rough. He popped the hood, listening,

then hung a trouble light in the wild cherry
and bent to work under that bright canopy.

The Big Jew

for Peter Perez

Parlante drove a grocery truck. Bellows,
a hack. O'Brian's son got sent upstate.
Fitzgerald's arm ended in a hook below
his elbow—men who often shared the late

summer dusk as it brimmed and cooled, sitting
in someone's front yard where my father was
unwelcome, a friend from years ago revealing,
behind his back he was the *Big Jew* to neighbors.

Regret was my father's religion: his
football scholarship yanked for driving drunk,
his chilly, caustic wife, fat, secretive son.

Did my father ever stand at a dark screen,
hearing a cough, a curse, a pop top hissing
like an open airlock, someone laughing?

A Jew on a Picnic

That's what my girlfriend's father called me, that
whey-faced bank guard with his darkly oiled service

revolver: pushy, greedy, grasping, I got
the message. *Mocky. Kike. Sheeny. Shyster.*

My friend's grandmother was always in the yard,
tending tomatoes in her widow's weeds.

Morta Christo, she'd whisper if she saw me.
The old lady, he'd laugh, *says you killed God.*

I have an alibi, I likely said.
More than fifty years ago that eager

bank-dick's daughter and I tongued each cleft
and salt lick. I recall best *Jewboy, Hebe, Yid,*

the way her father's eyes so closely matched
the frayed, sweat-bleached blue of his shirt.

Triptych for MKF

Rose Mallow

Because we couldn't keep the sand from dancing
under the kitchen door when the wind was wrong—
and it was always wrong—our lives answered
to those laws that urged and toppled the modest dunes.

And when my mother couldn't coax flowers
from their beds, she fell in love with rose mallow,
and loved it best, those leggy, bright clusters
lodged among the reeds, scarlet or yellow.

Or did she love it only? The way it dimmed
and fired when weather-laden clouds lumbered
through. Regret sets a banquet for starvelings.
Most days were book-ended—redbreasts, redwings,

a covey of ducks breaking cover, black beads
on a broken string. Good years and bad.

Plein-Air

We knew that lightning was more likely to kill
our mother than a rattler when she wanted
to paint the wind roughing up the cattails,
green as new grass among last year's bronze.

My brother walked ahead, a 12-gauge resting
across his arm. I watched for snares and tussocks
that could take her down. Our mother was going
blind but still could see the water's restless

coinage, the tawny reeds' erratic rise
and drop. I didn't ask where he got the gun.
He returned the favor, not asking was I clean
and sober. Our mother's difficult boys

stood next to her, watching the tide drown
the strip of shore, the water measled with foam.

Plein-Air (again)

Toward the end she didn't paint as much
as doze under a five-and-dime sombrero,

her lawn chair turned to face the creek's broad mouth.
Uncluttered color fields—sky, bay, and marsh.

By then she couldn't discern the clamdigger's
smoke-colored shacks. One time she woke sorry

she'd never seen the Turner galleries
at the Tate. Another, glad her crazy kid sister

was dead and couldn't torment me. She was
awash in mutinous cells. There was nothing

we couldn't say. Her luminous watercolors
reminded me of Rothko. No, she explained:

It's much harder to paint what isn't there
than what is. And soon enough she wasn't there.

The Joys of Yiddish

When I came home from school a wad of Wrigley's
stuck to my hair, my bird-boned grandmother

who only spoke in Yiddish during the nightly
news, with its roster of *ligners* and *momzers*—

liars and bastards—cursed the kid who felt
I deserved to be adorned with flecks of spittle,

a slick badge of gum...*zol er mit di malekh
hamoves tokhter.* He should wed the Angel

of Death's daughter. Can a dead language
have a dead dialect? Not the shtetl schmaltz
of *Fiddler,* Cossacks dancing at the wedding

rather than raping the bride, no word
about the inescapable *vantzen,* the well-fed
bedbugs burrowed deep in the straw tick,

the horsehair or feathers. Not the borscht belt schtick
making Yiddish comfy for the goyim: *chutzpah,
goniff, gelt, kibitz, k'nish, kvetch,*

schlock, shlong, shtup. Not even its subtle
distinctions among fools and losers: *shlemazel, shlemiel,
shmegegge, shmendrik, shmo, shnook...*

What did the Jewish convicts speak
in the prisons of the tzar?

The conscripts posted to the eastern border,
plotting to kill their sergeant?

Shakedown artists, card sharps
who thrived in the Jewish Quarter?

Astrologers and other outcasts
banished by the rabbinic court?

Procurers trolling the market stalls
for girls on Shabbos errands?

How many with the eye unaided,
bright nail heads hammered in the night sky?
How many from the dark
road between Suvero and Ozerki,
along the Narev's braided channels?

How many Yiddish poems unwritten,
manuscripts unfinished, poets lost?
A star for each? Ten stars?
Beyond glitter. Beyond fierce haze. Beyond the sun
at noon zenith, every fact

stark and shadowless,
the distinct blades of grass, the rabbit's track
through the grain, skittery ripples
left by water striders in the rain barrel.
I can't speak Yiddish. Not a word,

though I've consulted the great dictionaries,
the guidebooks to the dead cities
and the cities of the dead.
Though I've studied the phone directory for the Jewish ghetto
on the Lower East Side.

Business listings for burial societies,
settlement houses, orphanages, charities
for unmarried girls starting
to show. If I could forgive I wouldn't
be a better Jew. I wouldn't be

a Jew at all. Bobby Muller's face
comes closer, masked in malice,
long and pointed as a fairytale goblin,
a bubble of spit on his lower lip.
Because we're the people of the book,

I'm not surprised when it starts
to char and smolder around the edges,
though I can still see the shallow
pockmark on his right cheek. I'm not
surprised when my grandmother starts to pray

in the one true tongue of the Jews,
the language of the gutter, of the oilcloth-
and-linoleum tenement kitchen,
the flour leavened with chalk and everyone
else asleep,

language of the stevedore
whose kidneys ache like a truss of fire,
the mystic starving himself to death
so he can die under the Divine Kiss.
I've written down

what I could. It's like a ransom note
in a noir gangster movie, words and letters
clipped from newspapers
and put to a more sinister purpose:
Er zol kak'n mit blit un mit aiter.

He should crap blood and pus.

Color by Number Picture of Auschwitz

The tower-turreted station, the open maw
that swallows the transports: blank. The suffocating,
padlocked cattle cars: blank. The retching, raw
fetor of urine, feces. The Nazi doctor using

one finger to cull the feeble from the crowd,
to winnow out the children. Left or right:
blank or blank. The taunting motto, *Arbeit
Macht Frei,* the Aryan idea of a joke.

The showers primed with pesticide: blank.
The Jewish work detail arranging corpses
face up, so they can pry the gold from their blank

mouths. The brickwork chimney casting its blank
shadow across the camp, a sundial for the
blank, blank, blank, blank, blank.

The Recording Angel

Out cold or dead, my mother's kid sister
lies on the floor, another botched attempt

at living clean, another botched attempt
at dying when the kneeling cop finds a

pulse. These rehearsals scar the heart. My aunt's.
My mother's. But my father's stingy pump

had nothing to give beyond a weak man's contempt
for weakness, for a sorry pill head who couldn't

manage to kill herself. There's an angel
of forgetting whose kisses are dry, delicate

as a grandmother's. There's one tasked with getting
it down decades after the trail went cold.

He writes and writes, chided and crossed by ghosts,
wings patched and heavy as an immigrant's coat.

Google Earth View of the House I Grew Up In

What hasn't changed? The coarse grass struggles still
for purchase. Up and down the dead end
the lawns are scuffed with thin patches, the sand
never far from the surface. Whoever holds

the mortgage has kept the front door Chinese red,
the color that so affronted my father. It was
one more of his arty wife's screwball ideas.
The pines are gone. All four shallow-rooted,

not long for this world. Yet nothing took them down,
not even the ice that broke the maple's spine.
Seedlings when I first saw the house at five.
Spires at fifty when I came to clean it out.

Standing at the windows they heard everything:
the daily churn and mutter, laughter, weeping.

***

Churn and mutter: the mouth shaping a column
of air into our first language: *family*—

that accent we can never shake or outrun —
the house sighing and talking in its sleep,

giving itself a little more to the wet.
The pines only allowed the sun to pass

in brilliant shards and splinters, casting a jagged
archipelago across the unbraiding rag

rug. The islands dimmed and drifted all day.
The light, otherwise, was subaqueous,

as if we lived at the bottom of a pond.
No, that's how it felt not how it was.

Not knowing the difference is one way
we lie to ourselves. In the kitchen the sun.

***

The kitchen sun hammered the table where
I did my homework—fierce enough some days
to blind me to the lines ruled on the paper—
where my father finally managed to pound algebra

through my thick skull. But after dark the room
shrank, even in summer, acres of crickets
going for broke in the cattails, the crescent
moon snagged in the screen. The double tubes

of fluorescent light found every flaw. The knots
trying to breathe through the paint. The brown-and-black
GI Bill linoleum that didn't show
the dirt. My mother listening to the radio,

her beloved opera. The lady of the house.
How little use she had for any of us.

***

My mother had no use for the dropouts and freaks
who were my friends. Savants who knew what gauge

guitar strings Hendrix played. A cop who dealt.
An angry wife fed up with working days.

My mother got so tired of us laughing
too loud in the kitchen, playing her radio,

she let me move my bed into the half-
finished room with the washer, dryer, soap.

I could count the sleek, tumescent eggplants the Greek
was growing, vines shot through with red peppers.

The view at night, the lights at the end of the street
backed by miles of dark—marsh, creek, bay, barrier

islands and at the last, the shawl-edged ocean
repeating the same sad story over and over.

***

Over and over. My mother never wearied
of telling me she didn't trust TJ.
Twins drawn to trouble, sharp-tongued soulmates.
How else could she explain the bales of weed

I blazed and burned? Ray-Bans and Zippos,
my chronic shoplifting? False dawn: The kitchen
window filling with ash, my mother walking in
on me and TJ boiling our works on the stove.

I wasn't sure if she was truly there.
We'd been skin-popping speed, needling the clever
muscles that flexed and pointed our fingers.
Hard-boiled eggs, Mrs. F, TJ told her.

The pan simmered and spat. I heard my mother
go back to bed, her give and take on the stairs.

***

How well I knew the stair's give and take: stoned
or drunk or half-hobbled with blue balls, stealth

by then was second nature. Up and down,
a cat burglar searching for something to steal.

In the bedroom that we shared my brother
built his model planes, combat-ready rows

of transports, fighter jets, Navy bombers
waiting for an enemy that never showed.

Grade-school grads back on a visit find
cavernous classrooms shrunk in scale, water

fountains waist high. When I remember right
the airy room dwindles: two beds, a dormered

window. Two brothers who spoke their own skewed
dialects, both some distance from the truth.

***

Perhaps the prime solace of distance: that
it doesn't change. An easy mistake. At first
the new houses were wooden cells, bare joists
and studs. Soon enough they became vista, backdrop.

But line of sight was just one loss. There was
no way to gauge how far, at least in miles,
we lived from Ocean Lea or Harbor Isle,
chi-chi enclaves with central air, station cars.

Memory allows no distance. Light falling
sixty years—a mossy turtle basking
on a log—takes no longer to reach us
than a Google image of the Doge's palace,

even as we float and fall through ourselves:
What hasn't changed? The coarse grass struggles still.

Stray Thoughts for Viktor Schlovsky

That winter the Hudson froze all the way
to Poughkeepsie. Battleship-gray icebreakers
kept a black channel open for the upriver
coal barges, as if they were running a blockade.

Something Russian about the cold, the stale
snow made me think of Schlovsky, my old
linguistics professor, whom Khrushchev furloughed
after four years in the Gulag. "They let out all

us 'spies' after Stalin died," he said. "Interesting facts,
if true," he scribbled on the cover of my senior thesis,
a study of vowels in colloquial phrases—
like *fuck or fight, shit or go blind*. But when I asked

weren't facts implicitly true, he warned me,
"Don't be an idiot, Mr. Fischer. Don't be naïve."

Rolling Stock for Marty Lampner

...where the Southern cross the Yellow Dog—W.C. Handy

The ways we choose to waste our time away
from work are equally slight, though mine has earned
the iffy cachet of art, all because I've learned
the ins and outs of a 16th century

lattice, while you're just playing with model trains.
I couldn't say who gains the greater joy
—which counts for all—your weedy spurs, trompe l'oiel
tricks, my attempts to mill the language down.

Two lives ago we sang about empty
freight cars, suburban naïfs juiced on elsewhere.
Build this for me in your workshop, two pairs

of rusted rails, that haunting junction Bessie
Smith called out, last stop for all loss, all love—
where the Southern cross the Yellow Dog.

Fax Machine Receives Message from God

I celebrate the supermarket tabs,
those inky, creased tabloids that rolled off the press
looking as if they'd already been read
and refolded—*Elvis Alive, Runs for Prez,*

Man's Head Explodes in Barber Chair. Consigned
to the checkout aisle, they blossomed like blowsy
newsprint flowers above the gum, candy,
Slim Jims. *Mermaid Cemetery Discovered.*

Penumbral impulse items—*Duck Hunters
Shoot Angel, Gay Aliens Found in UFO
Wreck*—stitched from hunches, toothaches, ghetto
dream books, *Computer Virus Kills Humans,*

what the phosphenes suggest when our eyes are shut.
The news is fake, and worse than we thought.

Ferry to Hart Island

Swapping out a single vowel changes the island's name
to "hurt," better suited to the city's potter's field, terminus
for its unclaimed dead, mapped to their mass graves,
where numbered coffins are stacked by shackled prisoners

in dayglo-green jumpsuits eager to work for 50 cents
an hour and a view of the East Bronx money can't buy.
Not just the homeless make landfall here, in these dense
underground tenements, strict trenches chiefly occupied

by acre after acre of the poor, a handful of well-heeled
second cousins and great aunts unlucky enough to outlive
their connections, a few hundred "on loan" to med schools
and teaching hospitals, in the chill lingo of the civil service.

Yet even here, where the million dead are legion, how little
headway they've made on the marsh grass, the tawny cattails.

Lust for Life (MGM: 1956)

The crows in the Van Gogh biopic with Kirk Douglas
deserve an Oscar for best supporting actor,
bedeviling and battering Vincent at his last plein-air
landscape. It's great box office,

but it's not true. His final work: the serene
Daubigny's Garden. Violet-bordered flower bed,
violet cat, his friend's wife framed by a blue-rinsed
stucco wall. Nothing throbs or threatens

to change shape.
                    No. Van Gogh has to suffer
for painting the wagon ruts through the wheat
apple green, the wind's yellow and rust shimmer.

The crows flap and jeer on cue. Vincent
scribbles a few black glyphs on the canvas, staggers
from the easel and puts a bullet in his gut.

Swallowtail and Killing Jar

It's not enough to stand in the crowded dark
applauding each concussive heart or burst,
ring or star before it frays to sparks,
not when the tubby kid in black lace-ups

and shorts, his muffin-top girlfriend turned out
in peasant blouse, come close to butting heads
at each incoming round, eager to show
they alone command the secret knowledge,

they alone have cracked the genetic code
and see every barrage for what it is,
not Uncle Sam and Honest Abe, not the gold
Liberty Bell, the crackling Old Glories,

but double petals, tourbillions, and garniture—
shop talk that tells the world there's more to you
than trig and chem, chess club and school paper.
It's not the young alone who hope minutiae

and obsession—superheroes, Pokémon,
or swallowtail and killing jar—will ease
the gluey shames and doubts of the quotidian,
the way a sudsy sponge cuts baked-on grease

in a TV commercial, will help shush
the dogged questions that echo at night along
the secret stairs wound within the nautilus:
Am I a queer? Am I ugly? What's wrong

with me? I was too other to be a nerd
in senior high, so long ago the ice
sheets slowly pulling back like pinsetters
in a bowling alley. Who was my tribe?

some freaks, apprentice felons nodding out
in Business Math, PM homeroom, a rabbit-eyed
albino who spoke so seldom he was thought
mute, a few tough girls who wore ID

bracelets with their boyfriend's names, frosted lipstick,
and always knew the best parties, the best
weed. What would I say to those two kids? Listen,
we share the same unstable components,

a tablespoon of aggrandizement, a tub
of self-pity. I've sailed under your flag,
your glum ensign, the shoals and silted-up
channels absent from the treacherous maps.

I'm almost an old man, staring down the double
barrels of seventy: The only cure for life
is life—square biz, honor bright—to recall
the dead patois of my predigital times.

But even then, you've got to be lucky.

This Call May Be Recorded for Quality-Assurance Purposes

When the customer-service rep says in her good
English she's "situated offshore," I ask what living
on an island is like. *With surfers and white sand?*
She answers in a bright, brittle voice, forcing

a smile in a foreign language, mistaking my joke
for a jibe. Her accent reminds me of white borscht
ladled over sausages, our waitress from some vague, sibilant
country—Latvia or Belarus, Moldova, Estonia.

I can ask for the menu in French, sound out a few lines
of Sappho, but I've never been any good at turning
words into money, unlike those eager kids scheduling

orders and hassle-free returns from a raw concrete
call center in the Eastern Bloc, clocks ticking off local time
in the U.S., empire of Christmas catalogs, Victoria's Secret.

Link Wray: One-Hit Wonder

one

Because he wanted his guitar to sound dirtier
than Elvis, dirtier than jazz or country and western,

dirtier than a grinding, slow dance at a record hop—
the boys' jeans bulging with ass-pocket pints of whisky,

the girls sweating Shalimar and Chantilly, cigarettes
tucked behind their ears like orchids.

Because nothing matched the jagged, fuzz-toned
music in his head, this full-blooded Shawnee,

who lost a year and his left lung to TB in the "death house,"
who knelt before Jesus as Fred Lincoln and rose up Link Wray

punched pencils in the cone of his cheap amp
and delivered "Rumble" and "Switchblade,"

"Crowbar" and "Jack the Ripper," each distorted note
nimbus-shrouded in noise.

two

"Rumble" sells four million copies, charts at No. 14.
Link buys his mother a house with real floors,

buys a two-toned leather jacket and matching penny loafers
mail order from Sears, buys a dinged and dented

'59 Caddie—shark-finned and black—
so the band can arrive at gigs in appropriate splendor:

opening a drive-in movie in Altoona, a ribbon cutting
at a shopping center in Daytona, bunting, red and white balloons,

where Link previews "Fatback,"
a dark tunnel of power chords that gets the kids dancing,

until the mayor tells him to shut it down.
Crisscrossing the bony ridge of the East Coast

to play bars and frat parties, clubs and county fairs,
Link selling albums from the trunk of the Wray-Mobile,

the record companies with names like condoms
—Trident, Superior, Scepter—going belly up.

Their big break: getting signed by a rock & roll revival,
20 minutes between Bill Haley and The Dixie Cups.

They play "Rumble" twice a night,
with an afternoon show on Sunday.

three

Link writes a song every day,
wrapped around his black and red Telecaster, bought on time,

in the Caddie's deep backseat: throwaways and novelty numbers
like "Run, Chicken, Run" and "Summer Dream,"

his reverb-drenched homage to surf music.
He tries gospel, but even the Christian radio stations

won't give airtime to "Fire and Brimstone,"
where the guitar and drums march lockstep

through hell, with Link chanting "fire, fire, fire" on the chorus.
The Wray-Men take a gig as the house band

at DC's 1023 Club, a squat cinderblock cave
built into the side of a hill,

just until they get their chops back.
One night he waves them silent, tells the scant crowd,

"I was playing rock & roll ten years before it had a name."
A few bikers and GIs who come for the cheap beer

hoot and whistle through their fingers.
"Play 'Rumble,'" someone shouts.

Homage to Samuel Johnson: 17 Gough Square

I knew he lived on Gough, but London had three—
Square, Court, and Place. I had his house by heart, though,

tall and narrow, a high dormer where he sat at a trestle table
in his greasy powdered wig, burning through

each day's available light, afflicted by the tics and spasms
that kept him from work as a teacher or private tutor,

transcribing the world word by word into his dictionary.
Not the murmuration of starlings he was too blind to see,

skirling and shape-shifting over the mansard roofs
and wet slate. Not the murmuration, but the *small, singing bird*

and its cameo in Shakespeare, not the inkhorn term,
but *snuff, smoke, iron,* and an entry for himself,

lexicographer—a harmless drudge.
I'd come here with my new bride on pilgrimage.

I knew what it was to be dirty and poor, the two
always paired, no matter what stories we tell ourselves,

to wring out my underwear and socks in the sink
and wear them to work the next day still damp,

to kite a check at the end of the month to buy groceries.
I too had been afflicted.

But we'd been up and down this particular Gough
a half-dozen times: a poured-concrete garage

on the one side, on the other a row of postwar houses,
dingy and prefab. Someone came out into his yard, taking pity

on two tourists. But when I told him who we were looking for
he shook his head with neighborly certainty,

"No Johnsons on this block," in an accent
that drove all vaudeville Cockneys from my head,

listening patiently while I explained,
looking down at his weedy front walk, then adding,

more in benediction than derision: "Sam Johnson,
never heard of him."

Days of 1981

one

I worked that year at a law office so far
downtown the building hulked above the city's

original, off-grid streets, so old they bore
the humble names of elementals and trees—

Stone, Water, Spruce, Pearl, Maiden, Pine ... It was
an awful place, almost out of Dickens,

where proofreaders were expected to address
the lawyers as Mr., Mrs., Miss, though none

of us wore green eyeshades or tugged a forelock
when they passed, crafting torts on dissolution,

certificates of existence. On darker days
we were the shadow-weight cannon fodder

who thronged Hades—pasty, caffeine-fueled shades
called back each morning by the minimum wage.

two

The job was bleak as the neighborhood then,
before the patisseries with their lacy,

cast-iron chairs, faux Lost Generation
cafes. On airy, blue-scrubbed Saturdays

the Greek's newspaper kiosk was cinched
with chains, Cedar Street tagged with broken birds,

confused by the glass towers. I'd work and listen
to the jazz station until my eyes blurred.

Some nights I'd order takeout, invite my ex.
We'd smoke and strip and screw on the thick carpet,

the burl-blossomed conference table, or watch
our knowing twins couple and come apart

in the gilt-wreathed mirrors meant for the moneyed gaze
of hedge-fund managers, heads of state.

Expatriate Elegy

(for Ilya Shifrin)

"Am I understandable?" you'd ask every three or four
sentences. Your English got better with each shot of vodka
I downed, though the only Russian I can remember
from those years—*nietzschevo,* a drinking song's loud chorus.

"Nothing, nothing, nothing!" we'd laugh and shout
and knock back another, your two bedrooms crowded
as a communal apartment in Moscow,
expat cab drivers, concert pianist, mournful au pair in brown.

I'm better at elegy than friendship. "Why did you disappear?"
you asked at my wedding. Ten years of expensive talk
and I still don't have an answer. Now you're a ghost,

a few telltale gestures growing less palpable each year,
a voice that barely cuts through the static.
Sing with me: *Nietzschevo, nietzschevo, nietzschevo.*

In Memoriam: SKM

A blue star, rayed like a child's drawing, blazed
on your belly; on your back, a skull
wreathed in dahlias for the Day of the Dead.
I'd known you two months, two years in hospital
time, we joked, out on pass from the locked ward,
in your mother's house, in your childhood bed—
narrow, pink, canopied—unchanged for a decade,
still guarded by plush toys and a sock puppet,

as if a 12-year-old you could find her way
home, unscarred by razors and cigarette burns,
unscathed by mood swings and mania,
so at last you could be a real girl, learning
to wear lipstick and kiss, dancing to the radio
with your best friends—ignorant and whole.

Crazy Eights

That's what my father called them, the blackfish
we caught on the troll, or tried to, because they'd drive you crazy,
three quick hits on the line—*bap, bap, bap*—and they'd strip
the bait off the hook. The last long days

of late summer, the chum's eddy and iridescent slick
on the water. My father was getting on
with the business of dying: one careful Schlitz
nursed through the afternoon, each rationed Winston

raising a shuddering cough. It was a relief to know nothing
would ever be right or resolved between us.
That left the purity of small talk. Anchor or drift?

Bloodworms or fiddlers? A buck on the first fish.
From the air you'd have seen two men sitting in a skiff,
following the shallow, forked channels among the tidal islands.

Clamdiggers

They were the last. They kept their secrets. Where
to dig the sweetest cherrystones or find
the densest clusters of blue mussels. The tide
dead low, a mesh bag with a couple beers

hanging from the gunnel. Pete's Clam Bar, Charlotte's
buying bushels of steamers, littlenecks,
the gulls piping and jeering above the dock,
the men shucking shells. Every day a knockoff

of the one before. World without end the priest
intoned at Mass. It ended soon enough.
What could they do but take the town's offer

on their single-wide trailers along the creek?
Among the trash that had to be hauled off,
the shallow skiffs their grandfathers planed and caulked.

A Love Supreme

one

The first time you came with me I thought
I'd done something wrong, "fuck, fuck, fuck,"
you said, then started to laugh. You schooled me—
a skinny-scruffy virgin with bad skin
whose mother worked in the school cafeteria,
who shared a room with his 12-year-old brother—
steering my hand to the coarse tangle of your sex,
guiding my mouth. You read Baudelaire aloud
in bed, translating for me, your leg crooked
over mine, the room perfumed with patchouli
and Right Guard. I had Blake's "Chimney Sweeper"
by heart. You can almost see my bedroom window
from here, I said, standing at yours,
pointing to the cramped cinderblock houses
where my friends' fierce, gum-snapping older sisters
were helping clear the tables so they could study
for licenses in electrolysis and cosmetology.
You turned me on to Coltrane's "A Love Supreme,"
playing the third section over and over,
so I could hear the piano ghosting back
those jagged Egyptian scales that squalled
and squawked from his tenor sax.

two

After graduation you went to Europe.
You sent me a postcard of Blake's house,
a tiny heart inked over the window
on the second floor, where he lodged
above a vendor of whalebone corsets,
one of Baudelaire's grave, with something written
in French. And then you were gone, busy packing

for college, too busy to come to the phone
your mother said, as if you'd vanished
under the glassy lip of the sea.

three

If you orphaned me from one world,
you gave me another. In Paris I searched the crowds
at the Louvre for the elegant oval of your face,
years after you might have been there, almost
finding you in a narrow-hipped Modigliani nude.
In London I wished I could have shown you
the greensward at Hampstead Heath, where Keats
and Coleridge shook hands, and went home
with a barmaid who had your sharp wit
and crossed herself before we went to bed.
In Venice, with its theater of low clouds—
finally traveling solo—I took a *vaporetto*
to San Michele, where I filched an ivy leaf
from Pound's grave and bought souvenir postcards
of the Grand Canal, the lilac and lemon awnings
on the tourist shops like carnival floats.
In the chalky dawn over Naxos, where Odysseus
put in, my wife and I stripped and swam out
to the sandbar, drops of water jeweling
the fine hair on her arms. Memory can be poison
or benediction. My children are older
than we were that summer, but I can still
taste you, still see you, a tiny figure,
smaller and more sharply etched each year.
And some nights, I can almost feel you
kissing your way down my stomach
to take me in your mouth.

My Shabby Afterlife

Tommy T this morning, Tommy the Traveler, crossing the shadow
bridge, one approach anchored in sleep, the other
in the world, saying again how matter is mostly empty space, so
we can learn to walk through walls. A bit player

at best. Or Big Mike, Miguel Grande, eyes close set,
as if he were a fox-familiar in a Japanese folktale, telling me
swami Muktananda could fly and shit rubies if he wanted—
a face in the chorus, more scenery than dramatis personae.

I know them for what they are, neither ghosts nor captives,
time travelers who flicker and blink into the present for no reason.
And for what they say about all of us,

how these who-knows-how-many shards and splinters
half recalled by someone—smile, smirk, and taunt—
this shabby afterlife all we're likely to be granted.

Last Laugh

Humor begins with the body and its byproducts—farts, turds,
semen, spittle, pee. The best part of you, we'd say in our pale
version of the dozens, dribbled down your father's leg. A full
professor once told me his colleague was so dumb

he couldn't pour piss out of a boot. But the joke's on us,
when our lungs are heavy as a waterlogged life jacket, and we gasp
through ShopRite, an O_2 cannister in tow. Is there an audience
for my sonnet, "Self-Portrait of the Poet Wearing a Catheter"?

How could I not love the Elizabethans, the way their poems
ping-pong between belly laughs and terror, scored to the iambic
bite and rasp of the spade? Or Samuel Pepys, scared limp
by London's Great Plague, recounting the iron-wheeled tumbrils

stacked with corpses in his diary, the plague pits, how he rallied
after a glass of claret at dinner to feel up his wife's lady's maid.

Howlin' Wolf at the Fillmore East, June 7, 1968

(for Robert Palmer, 1945 – 1997)

Three songs into the set and the Wolf—
sober-suited as an undertaker—is still sitting
on a hard-backed chair center stage,
one huge hand cupping the harp to his mouth
as if he's going to snack on it, one benchmade
size 16 rising and falling like a drop hammer,
his belly-deep growl pleading and threatening,
the corded tendons and veins bulging in his neck
as if each word were a stump that has to be winched
out of the earth; the grunts and falsetto moans
that cap the verses, part field holler,
part freight train: *wooo, wooo, wooo.*
By now the mostly white audience is mostly
on its feet, almost clapping on the beat,
while the Wolf stalks across the stage, shrugging
and rolling his shoulders like a heavyweight,
dropping to all fours and throwing his head back
on the last chorus of "Howlin' for my Darlin',"
while Willie Dixon leans into his standup bass
and Hubert Sumlin slashes out a guitar solo
that's all bite and sting. The Wolf's back
in his chair, trying to ease his kidneys
without letting the audience see: 300 shows
a year, a decade or so on the chitlin circuit
grinding out 10,000 miles per, bucking
and bouncing between Indianapolis and Cairo,
Shreveport and St. Pete in a prewar Pontiac bus
whose shocks were gone by V-E Day,
and it's no wonder his kidneys throb and ache.
They'll kill him in a few years, despite
his ferocious will, his cutting back to six songs a set,

the dialysis machine rolled into the studio
for his last sessions. The band snakes into a slow-drag
version of "Smokestack Lightnin'," the Wolf pointing
deep into the auditorium, the horn section rocking
side to side, and now—50 years after the club date—
I start to hear what's been there all along:
not the flatted thirds and fifths the jazzers borrowed
to build a language, but the steady, bone-jolting work
that goes into art.

Plague and Rumor (NY 1980)

At night the city trembled on the molten slate
of the Hudson, the river strobing red
and blue, squad cars and fire engines,
something always burning, scorched flake

and cinder, the siren's shrill call and response.
The city teetered on the cusp of plague and rumor—
private clubs screening snuff flicks, packs
of feral cats swarming strollers in the South Bronx.

From my midtown office I could watch skaters
on the ice at Rockefeller Center—part snow globe,
part diorama—the Art Deco Atlas balancing
the world of commerce on his shoulders.

Some nights, taking the A train home, a man
walked up and down the car on his knees, shirtless
and barefoot, back and face blistered
with AIDS sarcomas, as if a lamprey had battened

on his body. Did I ever sluice my spare change
into his cupped hands? One time, a woman wearing
a garbage bag like a tunic squatted between
the subway's closing doors at 125th, releasing

a stream of urine the color of green tea. It stank
and steamed in the February cold. When I got
to my stop, the plows had finally been through,
gouging and forcing the snow into huge banks.

Above them I saw the fog-colored lights
of the bridge, a scant handful of half-hearted stars
that offered neither solace nor redemption,
that promised nothing and delivered it.

Soutine's 'Still Life with Rayfish'

He started with Chardin's "The Ray," losing
the cat, startled guilty-fierce by someone
we'll never see who caught it pussy-footing

among the shucked oysters. That leaves nothing
animate in Soutine's painting: a wing, a wedge
of dead fish spilling its guts, a bottle shaped

like a woman's butt, a creepy-crawly face
formed by the ray's nostrils and mouth. All flesh
is meat, Soutine reminds us, essentially

impermanent, offal and incarnadine
jumble of vegetables alike. He held
no truck with Chardin's measured, mellow-murky

palette, reworking his own ferocious pigments
to snare the world's furious, fluid turbulence.

Guide to New Jersey

Archetypal East Coast suburb, without the obsessive
planning that makes Levittown look like a printed-

circuit board from the air. Meat-and-potatoes
architecture—low-slung ranches, split-levels perched

above a garage, a few fanciful, steep-gabled Tudors
fit for a bird watcher or small-time Mafiosi,

north Jersey's favorite sons. Each week, the bucket loaders
tear down a few more, reclaiming the property

for million-dollar McMansions, starter castles
with balustrades borrowed from a Venetian palazzo,

Endura-Stone columns flanking the entrance—
bad taste on a grander scale than the houses

they supplant—mortgaged, silent-majority brick. Only
their vanishing made them worth a second glance.

Feral Parrots, New Jersey

Lime-Jell-O green and buff, brilliance beyond
the local candescent cardinals, strident jays
in their dress blues who scold and vex the day.
Aliens and strays. With a doubtful origin:

Some careless cargo-handler astonished, as
a plume of parrots funneled from the box
he dropped. Doubtful. Unwanted pets who flock
across the Hudson from the Latinx Heights

more likely. But though the birds are borderless
they share a nomad home: hunger, which is
everywhere under the sky. They roil and trail

behind the mower, scissoring worms, crickets,
skull-white grubs—dun-feathered, burnt-match, raucous-
colored as Fiestaware at a garage sale.

Fort Hudson, New Jersey

Someone in this leafy subdivision, where the lawn service
plants yellow pennants when they spray weed killer,
whips her son's bare legs and butt

with a lamp cord, while he cups his slight cock and balls.
Someone yanks the louvered blinds closed,
knocks his wife to her knees and prizes her mouth open.

But when the woman drives to the ER wearing a mask
of bruises, or a gym teacher calls Family Services,
the local news rolls a truck, shoots the front yard

wishing well, the Chinese lions with permed manes,
as if to implicate this tidy brick neighborhood,
all of us good neighbors, minding our business.

Night Piece: New Jersey

This far north there's not much
dark, where the state's broken flint

arrowhead would be fitted
to the haft, where

acres of refineries glare
like small cities on

the horizon, joined
by the turnpike's

dazzling river, flare stacks
topped with flame—cobalt,

yolk, white, depending on the crude
being processed. After

the last customer
goes home, the one who lost

her keys and had to call
an Uber, after the night

crew stows the burnisher,
the walk-behind waxer

in the van, the mall
parking lot is shadowless

as a prison yard. Jersey's
famed barns glow and glitter

all night—Pottery, Tool,
Dress, Candy, Bed, Furniture,

Music—gaudy boxes of
brilliants. And cobra-

hooded security lights buzz
and flicker, flicker and burn

blue-green outside Whole
Foods and Costco, alchemical

fires doubled in the emergency
doors, while diners serve

breakfast round the clock,
the Tick Tock and Times

Square, counters gleaming,
spoons lying on their backs

at the Alibi, bright teardrops
at the bottom of their bowls

that could pass for stars,
if we could see the stars.

Suburban Sonnet

The rangy bleeding heart planted too deep
in shade, a scalloped concrete birdbath held
aloft by seahorses, its clientele
common as weeds—cardinals, jays, chickadees,

and mockingbirds. A squabble of grackles
splashes the basin dry, while sparrows scour
the chaff and seeds scattered from the feeder—
fallout from hyperactive gray squirrels.

Aromatic smoke, redolent of burning fat,
mesquite and hickory, lighter fluid, climbs
from a thousand, thousand propane grills, backyard

barbecues, charcoal briquettes precisely packed
as garden pavers. Let the offerings from
these altars find some favor with the gods.

Shakespeare in South Jersey

We'd already shot a tipsy round of
miniature golf, studied the postcards in
their revolving rack—the slender, red-

tipped lighthouse like a candy
cigarette, colony of white egrets sacked
out in a tree like furled umbrellas.

At the Seafood Shack, a flyer for
A Midsummer Night's Dream partly
covered by ads for septic tanks and used

jet skis. The worst Shakespeare I'd ever seen,
a hipster, East Village *Hamlet,* his father's
ghost played by a black man wearing a

stormtrooper helmet, motorcycle jacket
tricked out with rivets and zippers,
so I knew enough to keep my mouth

shut when Theseus wooed his Amazon
queen-captive in pure, vowel-swallowing
Jersey, or Bottom had to prop in place

the papier-mâché donkey's head gifted him
by Puck, that airy sprite with biceps
like a boxer. Yet this risible effort—

more than the sum of its flaws—
restored Shakespeare to the volunteer
fireman, the special-ed teacher,

so they could struggle with this mashup
of bedroom farce and fairy tale in
a drafty high school gym.

Fats Waller: Living Large

You made it look supremely easy, your
signature derby rakishly set, playing

for laughs—deft wisecracks, one-liners

that were a kind of jazz themselves, offered
ad lib, *One never knows, do one?* And all

the while your tireless, seven-league left hand

improvised sly clusters of tenths and triads
that wowed the swells at the Cotton Club and Smalls.

You lived large: bootleg by the gallon, veal

and ribeye and parfait always, a three-day
binge with Al Capone, kidnapped to play

his black-tie bash. Your enlarged heart rebelled

aboard the Super Chief, the Kansas City line,
on your way home to Harlem. You were 39.

Baltimore Christmas: Remembering Uncle Beanie

My ex's uncle. I was an *X* as well,
an unknown among nicknames, slights, envy, love—

aunts sneaking drinks behind mama's ample
Southern Baptist back. Beanie taking cover

in the spare bedroom when I ducked in, velvet-
voiced Gentleman Jim Reeves on the boombox.

Of course I knew. Sign. Countersign. Debate
over the deep-fathomed disputes: Was pop

music ruining Nashville? Could Tammy
or Loretta lay a finger on Patsy Cline?

I didn't see another Christmas. Beanie's
two boys, I heard, got into trouble—Vicodin,

Oxy—stumbling toward *X*'s of their own,
and all the heartbreak of a country song.

Thank You for Your Service

It's my beard of course, long and luxuriant as Whitman's
in those cabinet photos he gave to visitors.
More realistically, a Hasid in sneakers
and sweats. Santa, I expected, or Gandalf, not the man

in ShopRite who reached across his cart, with its payload
of bad choices—sausage patties, crinkle-cut fries—
to shake my hand. Or the one in the dry
cleaners, or waiting to pick up my order at Saigon Jade.

Right war—Viet Nam—wrong army, I don't tell them,
keeping it simple: "I'm not a vet," I say with a smile.
It's easy to thank me, a guy with a stringy ponytail
shopping at Home Depot. But which of us will commend

for his service the black man in jungle camo on patrol
in the bus station, or the one crashed out in the toilet stall?

On His Deafness

It hasn't taken music yet. It will
in time, degrading what the birds don't say—
open the door, the door, teakettle, teakettle—

the ragged rasp of *John the Revelator,*
Blind Willie Johnson's end-time call-and-response,
the slide's jagged scrimshaw incised on bone,

or Spooky Tooth's sustain-and-fuzz homage
to *Sgt. Pepper,* which sounds the way being stoned
on hash feels. My wife and kids are right, I should

do something, but there have been so many doctors:
my heart, my teeth, my eyes, my privates, my mind.
No doubt this failing can wait a little longer,

while I still can hear schoolchildren break and surge
across the street, sandpipers dodging the surf.

Night Blindness

They warned me this would happen when I was
dropping all that acid in '69 and '70, as if anyone
could predict in fifty years the blue margins
of the road at dusk would look coarse as

oatmeal, the windshield fill with dark until
I was peering through the porthole of a bathysphere,
the headlights of oncoming traffic globed phosphor,
like the lures trailed by those warty goblins living a mile

below the ocean's surface. I had more pressing problems
then, a summer gone missing. I could remember
sitting in my car, windows down, smoking a joint before
clocking in at Kroger's. Then it was autumn,

my sweater sleeve unraveled, the immaculate sun
buffing the car's hood, chrome, the acid just coming on.

Reverend Gary Davis: Live at Newport

I don't know what brings you to the brink of belief,
or even if you need to be brought. I don't know how easily
you slip into the garments of the saved. This music, for me,
is what faith sounds like: Blind Gary's voice grainy

and gruff from years of street singing above the mutter
of traffic, years of shouting in Harlem's sanctified
storefront churches, the folding chairs knocked over
when the Black women stand and testify.

But it's the guitar that delivers the keys to the kingdom:
the right hand threading the bass line through
the song, the left preaching barrelhouse and ragtime,
the reverend promising what I wish were the solid truth:

Well I've got fiery fingers, I've got fiery hands,
and when I get up in heaven, gonna join in that fiery band.

Oranges and Lemons

Honeymoon-giddy, almost lightheaded with being
in London my first time, the city like a promise redeemed,
"the brave, old, melancholy color," Henry James' close reading
of the porous, soot-scoured skyline, the nursery rhyme

churches and bells, St. Martin's and Bow, the antic,
venerable carnage at Covent Garden, where Mr. Punch laid low
Judy and baby and beadle, an incarnadine Old Nick—
"That's the way to do it," he prated and crowed.

All those books I buried my nose in
when I was meant to master something useful:
How glorious for us to be thronged by such companionable
ghosts, to climb to the garret where Dr. Johnson

set the English language right, or stand where Donne
woke too early with his lover and scolded the rising sun.

Aubade for LR

In squares of sun, sheened with sweat, we drift
and doze, stealing time meant for chores
for another chance to lie in bed and kiss,
misusing the day behind this closed door.

We are no longer lovely. We are all
that time has done to us in thirty years:
scar, suture, sag, belly, breast—all
those insults that mark us as survivors.

The light is coming on. The roses you cut
yesterday are shedding their heavy petals.
Let them snow over the bed, over our battered,

beautiful bodies. We know the price of indolence,
but lie a bit longer beside me. Let the work wait,
while there are mornings like this still to savor.

About the author

Aaron Fischer worked for 40 years as a print and online editor for newspapers and magazines. His poems have appeared in the *American Journal of Poetry, Briar Cliff Review, Crosswinds Poetry Journal, Five Points, Hudson Review, Naugatuck River Review,* and elsewhere. He won the 2020 Prime Number Magazine poetry contest, as well as the Top Sonnet award from the Maria W. Faust Sonnet Contest for 2019 and 2021. His chapbook, *Black Stars of Blood: The Weegee Poems,* comprises ekphrastic poems based on the work of the great news photographer of the '30s and '40s. Fischer was the founding rhythm guitarist of *Trayf,* the Jewish punk band.

www.ingramcontent.com/pod-product-compliance
Lightning Source LLC
Chambersburg PA
CBHW070512090426
42735CB00012B/2752